GW00374658

Other Helen Exley Giftbooks

A Special Gift of Wisdom (*in this series*)
Be What You Believe In
Words on Hope
...And Wisdom Comes Quietly
Inspirations A Book to Make Your Own

Published simultaneously in 2003 by Exley Publications Ltd
in Great Britain, and Exley Publications LLC in the USA.

2 4 6 8 10 12 11 9 7 5 3 1

ISBN 1-86187-542-8

Edited by Helen Exley.
Illustrated by Juliette Clarke.

Printed in China.

Exley Publications Ltd,
16 Chalk Hill, Watford, Herts WD19 4BG, UK

Exley Publications LLC,
185 Main Street, Spencer, MA 01562, USA

www.helenexleygiftbooks.com

Bulk copies of this book are available at special discounts for promotional purposes,
and for charity fundraising. Please contact *Dept P. Special Sales* for details.

A SPECIAL GIFT
INSPIRATIONS

Illustrated by Juliette Clarke
A HELEN EXLEY GIFTBOOK

PUT IN EVERYTHING YOU'VE GOT

Life is a great big canvas;
throw all the paint on it you can.

DANNY KAYE (1913-1987)

Whatever you attempt,
go at it with spirit. Put some in!

DAVID STARR JORDAN (1851-1931)

It had long since come to my attention that
people of accomplishment rarely sat back
and let things happen to them.
They went out and happened *to* things.

ELINOR SMITH

Jump into the middle of things, get your
hands dirty, fall flat on your face, and then
reach for the stars.

JOAN L. CURCIO

THERE ARE NO SHORTCUTS
TO ANY PLACE WORTH GOING.

BEVERLEY SILLS, B.1929

BEGINNINGS

Don't be afraid of the space between your dreams and reality. If you can dream it, you can make it so.

BELVA DAVIS

We cannot discover new oceans unless we have the courage to lose sight of the shore.

AUTHOR UNKNOWN

You may never know what results come from your action. But if you do nothing, there will be no result.

MAHATMA GANDHI (1869-1948)

I ALWAYS BELIEVED THAT IF YOU SET OUT TO BE SUCCESSFUL, THEN YOU ALREADY WERE.

KATHERINE DUNHAM, AT THE AGE OF 81, B.1912

Far away there in the sunshine are my highest aspirations. I may not reach them, but I can look up and see their beauty, believe in them, and try to follow where they lead.

LOUISA MAY ALCOTT (1832-1888)

Start by doing what's necessary, then what's possible and suddenly you are doing the impossible.

ST. FRANCIS OF ASSISI (1181-1226)

DO IT NOW!

Whatever you can do,
or dream you can, begin it.

JOHANN WOLFGANG VON GOETHE (1749-1832)

...IF NOW IS NOT THE TIME TO ACT, WHEN WILL IT BE?

HILLEL, c.50 A.D.

Are you in earnest? Then seize this very minute. Boldness has genius, power and magic in it; only engage and then the mind grows heated. Begin, and then the work will be completed.

JOHANN WOLFGANG VON GOETHE (1749-1832)

The only joy in the world is to begin.

CESARE PAVESE (1908-1950)

*All growth
is a leap
in the dark.*

HENRY MILLER
(1891-1980)

GROW, CHANGE, SOAR...

Dare to Grow: Dare to Dream.

PAM BROWN, B.1928

*Change gives us branches, letting us
stretch and grow and reach new heights.*

PAULINE R. KEZER

*Challenges make you discover things about
yourself that you never really knew.
They're what make the instrument stretch
– what make you go beyond the norm.*

CICELY TYSON, B.1933

*I thought I'd take style to its limit....
My philosophy is a belief in magic,
good luck, self-confidence and pride.*

GRACE JONES, B.1952

...TO FILL THE HOUR!

WAKE UP WITH A SMILE AND GO AFTER LIFE... LIVE IT, ENJOY IT, TASTE IT, SMELL IT, FEEL IT.

JOE KNAPP

To fill the hour – that is happiness;
to fill the hour, and leave no crevice for
a repentance or an approval.

RALPH WALDO EMERSON (1803-1882)

Fill each day. Give it your youth, your health, your abilities, your hope – so that your whole life will be a wonder. And your memories sweet.

PAM BROWN, B.1928

A new life begins for us with every second. Let us go forward joyously to meet it. We must press on, whether we will or no, and we shall walk better with our eyes before us than with them ever cast behind.

JEROME K. JEROME (1859-1927)

DO IT! BELIEVE IT!

*Nothing on earth is more gladdening
than knowing we must roll up our sleeves
and move back the boundaries
of the humanly possible once more.*

ANNIE DILLARD, B.1945

*Progress results only from the fact that there
are some men and women who refuse
to believe that what they know to be right
cannot be done.*

RUSSELL W. DAVENPORT

WE HAVE ENOUGH PEOPLE
WHO TELL IT LIKE IT IS — NOW WE COULD USE
A FEW WHO TELL IT LIKE IT CAN BE.

ROBERT ORBEN, B.1927

The one with courage is a majority.

ANDREW JACKSON (1767-1845)

Make voyages. Attempt them.
There's nothing else.

TENNESSEE WILLIAMS (1911-1983)

GO FOR IT

*All our dreams can come true –
if we have the courage to pursue them.*

WALT DISNEY (1901-1966)

*You miss a hundred percent of the shots
you never take.*

WAYNE GRETSKY, B.1961

*SHOOT FOR THE MOON. EVEN IF YOU MISS IT
YOU WILL LAND AMONG THE STARS.*

LES BROWN

*knowledge of the path cannot be substituted
for putting one foot in front of the other.*

M.C. RICHARDS

*Who wanted to creep along in comfort when
there was one chance in a thousand of flying?*

GAIL GODWIN, B.1937

MAKE NO LITTLE PLANS

Make no little plans;
they have no magic....
Make big plans,
aim high in hope and work.

DANIEL H. BURNHAM

Plunge boldly into the thick of life!

JOHANN WOLFGANG VON GOETHE (1749-1832)

*Go confidently in the direction of your
dreams! Live the life you've imagined.*

HENRY DAVID THOREAU (1817-1862)

*Throw your heart out in front of you
And run ahead to catch it.*

ARABIC PROVERB

Don't be afraid to take big steps. You can't cross a chasm in two small jumps.

DAVID LLOYD GEORGE (1863-1945)

I think that wherever your journey takes you, there are new gods waiting there, with divine patience – and laughter.

SUSAN M. WATKINS, B.1945

BELIEVE YOU CAN

Believe you can and you can.
Believe you will and you will.
See yourself achieving,
and you will achieve....

GARDNER HUNTING

WHAT WE VIVIDLY IMAGINE, ARDENTLY
DESIRE, ENTHUSIASTICALLY ACT UPON,
MUST INEVITABLY COME TO PASS.

COLIN P. SISSON

You can have anything you want if you want
it desperately enough. You must want it with
an exuberance that erupts through the skin
and joins the energy that created the world.

SHEILA GRAHAM

Believe as though you are,
and you will be....

ERNEST HOLMES (1887-1960)

Each new day is an opportunity to start all over again... to clarify our vision.

JO PETTY, FROM "AN APPLE A DAY"

When old words die out on the tongue, new melodies break forth from the heart....

RABINDRANATH TAGORE (1861-1941)

TRY AGAIN. FAIL AGAIN. FAIL BETTER.

SAMUEL BECKETT (1906-1989), FROM "WORSTWARD HO"

No matter what happens,
keep on beginning and failing.
Each time you fail,
start all over again,
and you will grow stronger
until you find that you have
accomplished a purpose....

ANNE SULLIVAN

THROUGH BAD TIMES WE GROW, WE FIND STRENGTH

Walls have been built against us, but we are always fighting to tear them down, and in the fighting, we grow, we find new strength, new scope.

ESLANDA GODE ROBESON

You should nurse your dreams and protect them through bad times and tough times to the sunshine and light which always come.

WOODROW WILSON (1856-1924)

We are all in the gutter, but some of us are looking at the stars.

OSCAR WILDE (1854-1900),
FROM "LADY WINDERMERE'S FAN"

WINTER IS ON MY HEAD,
BUT ETERNAL SPRING
IS IN MY HEART.

VICTOR HUGO (1802-1885)

Meet the future with hope and courage, enthusiasm, energy and joy. From them build a life that's worth the living.

PAM BROWN, B.1928

KEEP ON, KEEP GOING

*Follow your dream... take one step at a time
and don't settle for less, just continue to climb.*

AMANDA BRADLEY

ONE STEP – CHOOSING A GOAL
AND STICKING TO IT –
CHANGES EVERYTHING.

SCOTT REED

*WHEN NOTHING SEEMS TO HELP, I GO
AND LOOK AT A STONECUTTER HAMMERING
AWAY AT HIS ROCK PERHAPS A HUNDRED
TIMES WITHOUT AS MUCH AS A CRACK
SHOWING IN IT. YET AT THE HUNDRED AND
FIRST BLOW IT WILL SPLIT IN TWO, AND I KNOW
IT WAS NOT THAT BLOW THAT
DID IT, BUT ALL THAT HAD GONE BEFORE.*

JACOB RIIS (1849-1914)

...if you want something very badly, you can achieve it. It may take patience, very hard work, a real struggle, and a long time; but it can be done. That much faith is a prerequisite of any undertaking.

MARGO JONES (1913-1955)

LIVE! SEIZE THE DAY!

*I don't want to get to the end of my life
and find that I lived just the length of it.
I want to have lived the width of it as well.*

DIANE ACKERMAN, IN "NEWSWEEK"

But warm, eager, living life
– to learn, to desire to know, to feel,
to think, to act.
That is what I want. And nothing else.

KATHERINE MANSFIELD (1888-1923),
FROM HER "JOURNAL"

*Whatever you do, do it
with all your heart and soul.*

BERNARD BARUCH (1870-1965)

Life is too short to be small.

BENJAMIN DISRAELI (1804-1881)

THERE ARE ONLY TWO WAYS
TO LIVE YOUR LIFE.
ONE IS AS THOUGH NOTHING
IS A MIRACLE.
THE OTHER IS AS THOUGH
EVERYTHING IS A MIRACLE.

ALBERT EINSTEIN (1879-1955)

YOU ALONE

I am only one,
But still I am one.
I cannot do everything,
But still I can do something;
And because I cannot do everything
I will not refuse to do
the something that I can do.

EDWARD E. HALE (1822-1909)

DON'T LET YOUR SPECIAL
CHARACTER AND VALUES,
THE SECRET THAT YOU KNOW AND
NO ONE ELSE DOES, THE TRUTH —
DON'T LET THAT
GET SWALLOWED UP BY THE GREAT
CHEWING COMPLACENCY.

MERYL STREEP, B.1949

FLYING FREE

No bird soars too high,
if he soars
with his own wings.

WILLIAM BLAKE (1757-1827),
FROM "THE MARRIAGE OF HEAVEN AND HELL"

My will shall shape my future.
Whether I fail or succeed shall be no
one's doing but my own. I am
the force; I can clear any obstacle before
me or I can be lost in the maze.
My choice; my responsibility; win or lose,
only I hold the key to my destiny.

ELAINE MAXWELL

NOW THE REAL BEGINNINGS OF THE
"FREEDOM" ...COMING AFTER SO MANY
YEARS OF REACHING OUTWARD FOR IT
— TO FINALLY DISCOVER ALL I HAD TO DO
WAS REACH INWARD, AND IT WAS
THERE WAITING ALL THE TIME FOR ME!

ALISA WELLS

LIFE FIRE

*To burn always with this hard
gem-like flame. To maintain this
ecstasy, is success in life.*

WALTER PATER (1839-1894)

THIS FIRE IN ME...
IT'S THE HUNGER OF ALL
MY PEOPLE BACK OF ME,
FROM ALL AGES, FOR LIGHT,
FOR THE LIFE HIGHER!

ANZIA YEZIERSKA
(c.1885-1970)

*I will never abdicate.
I shall always want everything.*

MARIE LENÉRU

OUTWARD BOUND

Do not follow where the path may lead.
Go, instead, where there is no path
and leave a trail.

AUTHOR UNKNOWN

One doesn't discover new lands
without consenting to lose sight of the shore
for a very long time.

ANDRÉ GIDE (1869-1951)

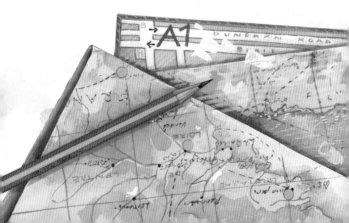

If you come to a fork in the road, take it.

YOGI BERRA, B.1925

The only way of finding the limits
of the possible is by going beyond them
into the impossible.

ARTHUR C. CLARKE, B.1917

It is not easy to be a pioneer – but oh,
it is fascinating! I would not trade
one moment; even the worst moment,
for all the riches in the world.

ELIZABETH BLACKWELL (1821-1910)

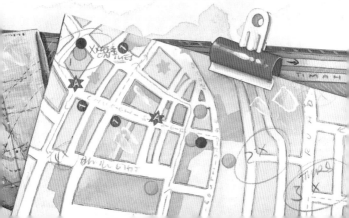

IT IS NOT TOO LATE

*It seems to me that we can never give up
longing and wishing while we are
thoroughly alive. There are certain things
we feel to be beautiful and good,
and we must hunger after them.*

GEORGE ELIOT (MARY ANN EVANS)
(1819-1880), FROM "THE MILL ON THE FLOSS"

THERE IS NO GOOD REASON WHY
WE SHOULD NOT DEVELOP AND CHANGE
UNTIL THE LAST DAY WE LIVE.

KAREN HORNEY (1885-1952)

*Even if I knew certainly the world
would end tomorrow, I would plant
an apple tree today.*

MARTIN LUTHER (1483-1546)

It's a very short trip. While alive, live!

MALCOLM S. FORBES (1919-1990)

FOLLOW WHAT YOU LOVE

Follow what you love!... Don't deign
to ask what "they" are looking for out there.
Ask what you have inside.
Follow not your interests, which change,
but what you are and what you love,
which will and should not change.

GEORGIE ANNE GEYER

YOU ARE EVERYTHING THAT IS,
YOUR THOUGHTS, YOUR LIFE,
YOUR DREAMS COME TRUE.
YOU ARE EVERYTHING YOU CHOOSE
TO BE. YOU ARE AS UNLIMITED
AS THE ENDLESS UNIVERSE.

SHAD HELMSTETTER

*Never fail yourself
Never commit to limits...
Follow the particulars
of your spirit
as they pull you...*

VERONICA D. CUNNINGHAM

HOPES AND DREAMS

*I've dreamt in my life dreams that have stayed
with me ever after, and changed my ideas:
they've gone through and through me, like
wine through water, and altered the colour
of my mind.*

EMILY BRONTË (1818-1848)

You see things; and you say, "Why?"
But I dream things that never were;
and I say "Why not?"

GEORGE BERNARD SHAW (1856-1950)

Imagination is the highest kite one can fly.

LAUREN BACALL, B.1924

When you cease to dream you cease to live.

MALCOLM S. FORBES (1919-1990)

ALL PEOPLE WHO HAVE ACHIEVED GREAT THINGS HAVE BEEN DREAMERS.

ORISON SWETT MARDEN (1850-1924)

It is not a disgrace not to reach the stars,
but it is a disgrace to have no stars to reach.

BENJAMIN MAYS (1894-1984)

What is a *Helen Exley Giftbook*?

Helen Exley has been creating giftbooks for twenty-seven years, and her readers have bought forty-eight million copies of her works in over thirty languages. Because her books are all bought as gifts, she spares no expense in making sure that each book is as thoughtful and meaningful a gift as it is possible to create: good to give, good to receive. Helen's books strongly reflect the major concerns of her life; those of family relationships, wisdom and values.

Team members help to find thoughtful quotations from literally hundreds of sources, and the books are then personally created. With infinite care, Helen Exley ensures that each illustration matches each quotation, that each spread is individually designed to enhance the feeling of the words, and that the whole book has real depth and meaning.

You have the result in your hands. If you have loved it – tell others! There is no power on earth like the word-of-mouth recommendation of friends.

Helen Exley Giftbooks
16 Chalk Hill, Watford, Herts WD19 4BG, UK
185 Main Street, Spencer, MA 01562, USA
www.helenexleygiftbooks.com

Acknowledgements: The publishers are grateful for permission to reproduce copyright material. Whilst every reasonable effort has been made to trace copyright holders, we would be pleased to hear from any not here acknowledged. GEORGE BERNARD SHAW: Extract from *Back to Methuselah*. Used by permission of the Society of Authors, on behalf of the Bernard Shaw Estate. PAM BROWN: published with permission © Helen Exley 2003.